CHICKS & CHICKENS

HOLIDAY HOUSE
NEW YORK

BY **GAIL GIBBONS**

TO SARAH HIPSHER

Special thanks to Dr. Michael Opitz
of the Animal Veterinary Sciences Department
of the University of Maine, Orono, Maine.

Copyright © 2003 by Gail Gibbons
All rights reserved
Printed and Bound in December 2016 at Toppan Leefung
Dongguan City, China
www.holidayhouse.com
9 10
Library of Congress Cataloging-in-Publication Data
Gibbons, Gail
Chicks & Chickens/ by Gail Gibbons—1st ed.
p. cm.
Summary: An introduction to the physical characteristics, behavior,
and life cycle of chickens, as well as a dicussion of how chickens
are raised on farms.
ISBN 0-8234-1700-X (hardcover)
ISBN 0-8234-1939-8 (paperback)
1. Chickens—Juvenile literature. [1. Chickens.] I. Title.
SF487.5 .G53 2003
636.5—dc21
2002027472

ISBN-13: 978-0-8234-1700-1 (hardcover)
ISBN-13: 978-0-8234-1939-5 (paperback)

A ROOSTER is an adult male chicken.

A HEN is an adult female chicken.

A CHICK is a young chicken.

Chickens are birds. Birds sing in different ways. These are the ways that chickens sing.

"Cheep . . . cheep . . ."

"Cluck . . ."

"Cock-a-doodle-doo!"

DIFFERENCES BETWEEN CHICKS, HENS . . .

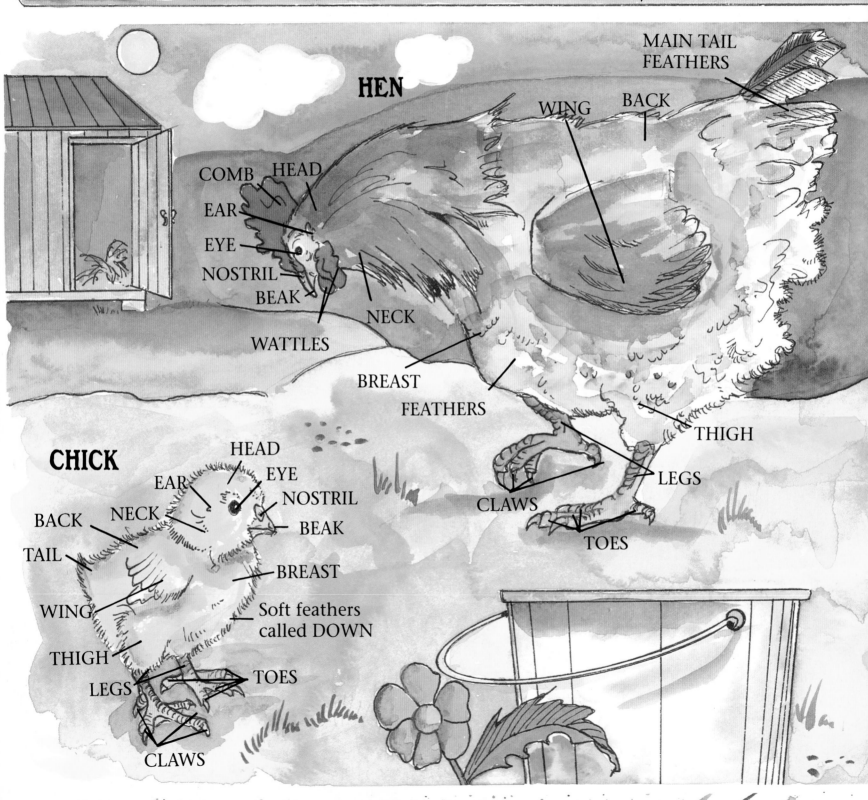

HEN

COMB
HEAD
EAR
EYE
NOSTRIL
BEAK
WATTLES
NECK
BREAST
FEATHERS
WING
BACK
MAIN TAIL
FEATHERS
THIGH
LEGS
CLAWS
TOES

CHICK

HEAD
EAR
EYE
NECK
NOSTRIL
BACK
BEAK
TAIL
WING
BREAST
Soft feathers
called DOWN
THIGH
LEGS
TOES
CLAWS

ROOSTER

COMB

EYE

EAR

HEAD

NECK

NOSTRIL

BEAK

WATTLES

SICKLE
FEATHERS

BACK

HACKLE
FEATHERS

BREAST

MAIN TAIL
FEATHERS

FEATHERS

WING

SPURS

LEGS

TOES

CLAWS

Chickens evolved from wild jungle fowl in Southeast Asia. They can't fly great distances because their wings are too weak.

People probably began to tame wild fowl for their eggs and meat during prehistoric times. Stories from China tell of people raising chickens about 4,000 years ago.

A BREED is a group of animals that shares many of the same features. In chickens it can be types of combs, skin colors, feather colors and patterns.

Today, many chickens are raised on farms. They lay eggs that people eat. Others are raised for their meat. There are about 113 different breeds of chickens.

A few chickens are raised as pets. Some chickens are entered in contests.

ROOSTERS OF SOME COMMON BREEDS.

BRAHMA

LEGHORN

CORNISH

NEW HAMPSHIRE

Roosters are more colorful than hens.

RHODE ISLAND RED

SUSSEX

POLISH

PLYMOUTH ROCK

Most breeds are named for the area where they were first developed. Depending on its breed, an adult chicken may weigh between 4 pounds (1.8 kg) and 10 pounds (4.5 kg).

A WATERER
on a small farm.

Chickens are always pecking and scratching at the ground, eating a little at a time. On small farms some owners let their chickens roam. They hunt for seeds, small plants, fruits, berries, insects, and worms. Because these chickens are able to move about freely, they are called free-range chickens.

CHICKEN FOOD is a dry mixture of corn, grains, meat, fish, vitamins, and minerals.

A WATERER on a large farm.

On large chicken farms, where chickens are raised in pens or cages, the owners feed the chickens chicken food. The chickens are always able to drink from waterers. In order for a chicken to drink water, it must toss its head back and let the water trickle down its throat.

CROP

STOMACH

GRIT

A GIZZARD has a
hard, thorny lining.

Chickens don't have teeth to chew their food. Instead, the food travels to a pouch in the throat called a crop. In the stomach the food mixes with digestive juices and enters the gizzard. The gizzard contains pieces of sand and small pebbles the chicken has eaten. These are called grit. The grit and the walls of the gizzard grind the food into small pieces.

PREENING

Chickens use their beaks to clean their feathers. This is called preening. They also take dust baths to get rid of any insects bothering them.

Chickens don't have a good sense of smell or taste. They do have good hearing. During the day, they have excellent eyesight.

When nighttime comes to a small farm, the chickens are put in a chicken coop. They sleep up on a perch. This is called roosting. Chickens don't have good night vision. Inside their coop they are safe from any nighttime enemies, such as weasels, foxes, and raccoons.

FLOCK

PECKING ORDER

Chickens prefer to be together in small groups called flocks. The leader pecks at the other chickens to let them know who is boss. That chicken is at the head of the pecking order.

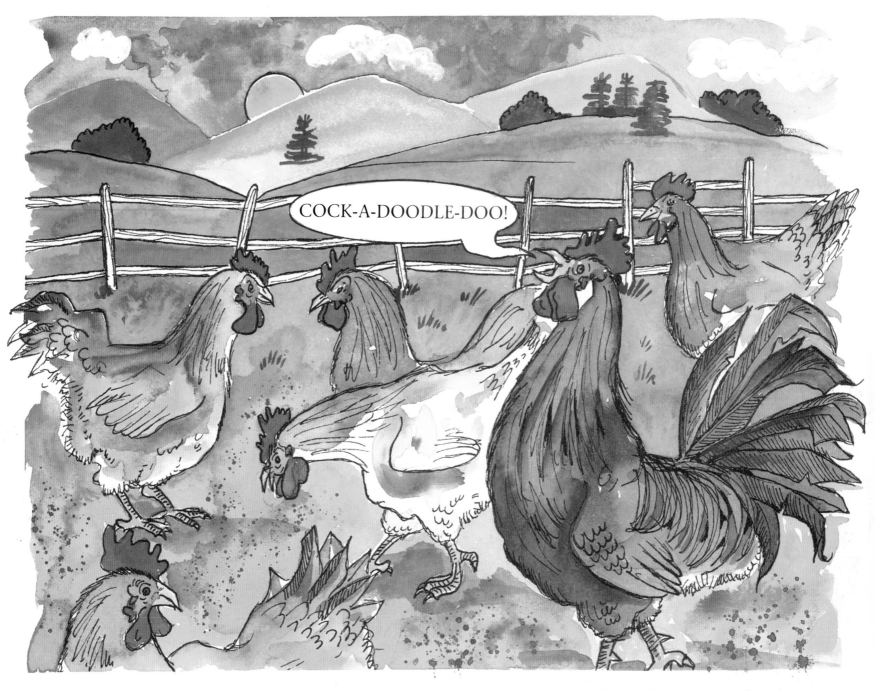

"Cock-a-doodle-doo!" This sound is often heard at dawn and in the evening. This sound, called crowing, is made by a rooster. A rooster usually watches over and protects a group of twelve to twenty hens. Roosters don't like other roosters and often fight each other.

ARAUCANA CHICKEN
(ARE·ah·con·ah)

6. From beginning to end, this process takes about 24 hours.

5. The hen lays her egg.

4. The SHELL forms.

3. The thin lining found inside an eggshell forms around the albumen.

2. ALBUMEN (al·BEW·men), the white fluid found inside an egg, is created in the oviduct.

OVARY

EGG CELL   OVIDUCT

1. EGG CELLS travel from the OVARY into the OVIDUCT.

Many farmers raise hens to lay eggs. Some breeds of hens lay white eggs. Others lay brown eggs. A few breeds lay green or blue eggs. A hen usually lays no more than one egg a day. Here is how it happens.

Eggs should be gathered from the nests in the chicken coop twice a day. This makes the hens want to keep laying eggs. During the winter, in cold climates, hens stop laying eggs until springtime. A rooster does not need to mate with a hen for her to lay eggs.

NEST

When a rooster mates with a hen, the egg cells inside her become fertile. After mating a hen prepares her nest by pulling twigs, feathers, bits of hay, and leaves around her.

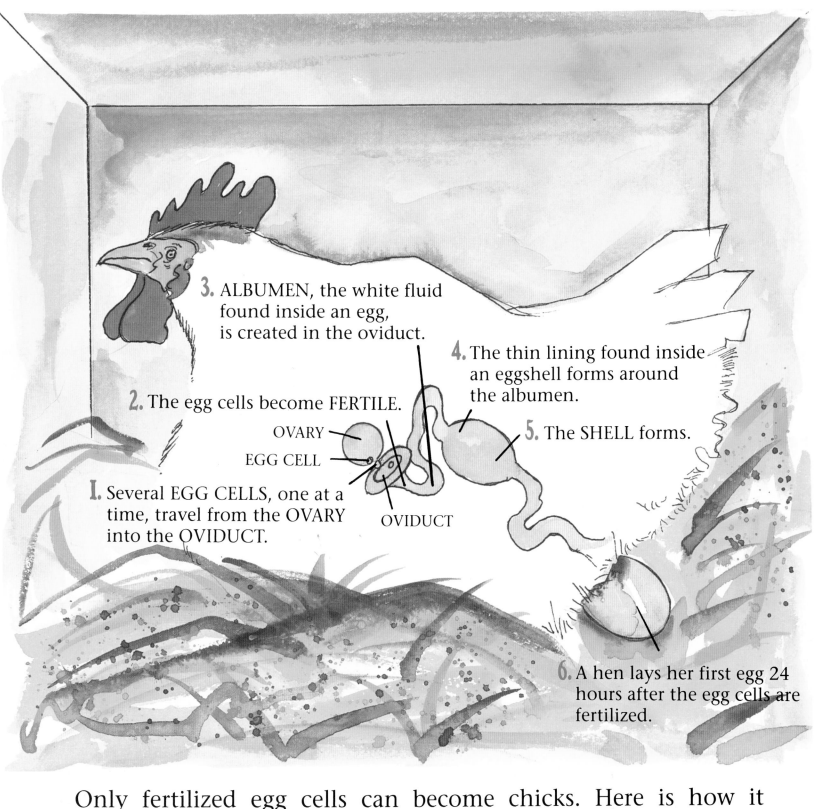

3. ALBUMEN, the white fluid found inside an egg, is created in the oviduct.

4. The thin lining found inside an eggshell forms around the albumen.

2. The egg cells become FERTILE.

OVARY

EGG CELL

5. The SHELL forms.

1. Several EGG CELLS, one at a time, travel from the OVARY into the OVIDUCT.

OVIDUCT

6. A hen lays her first egg 24 hours after the egg cells are fertilized.

Only fertilized egg cells can become chicks. Here is how it happens.

CLUTCH

INCUBATION

Each day the hen lays another egg. Usually there are six to twenty eggs. Any group of eggs in a nest is called a clutch. After the hen has laid all her eggs, she sits on them gently, turning the eggs over now and then, keeping them warm all over. Warming the eggs is called incubation.

An EMBRYO (EM·bree·o) starts to form on the yolk.

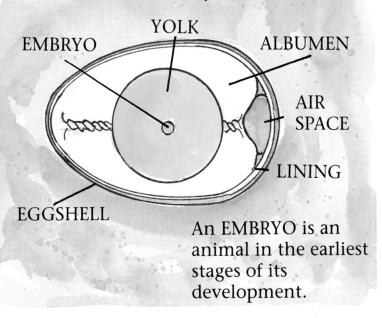

YOLK

EMBRYO

ALBUMEN

AIR SPACE

LINING

EGGSHELL

An EMBRYO is an animal in the earliest stages of its development.

BLOOD VESSELS spread over the yolk. Blood flows through them, carrying nutrients from the yolk to the embryo. The heart develops.

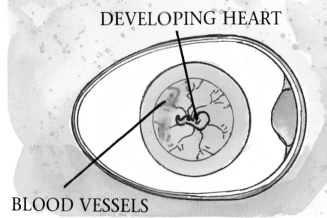

DEVELOPING HEART

BLOOD VESSELS

Now the embryo is surrounded by a water-filled SAC. As the embryo gets bigger, the yolk, its source of food, also gets bigger.

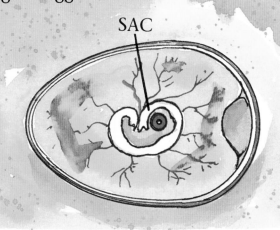

SAC

The embryo looks like a tiny bird.

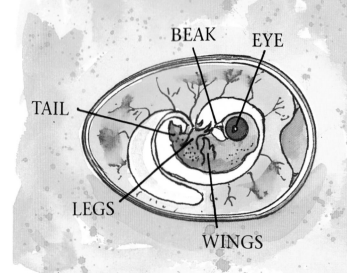

BEAK

EYE

TAIL

LEGS

WINGS

The mother hen incubates her eggs for about 3 weeks. During this time, a chick is growing inside each egg.

BROODING is the care given to an egg during incubation and the first 4 weeks after the chicks hatch.

HATCHING is when a chick breaks out of its shell.

The EGG TOOTH falls off shortly after the chick has hatched.

The first break in a shell is called a PIP.

When the incubated eggs are about 3 weeks old, the brooding mother hears a cheeping sound. The eggshell of one of the eggs begins to crack. A chick using its egg tooth, a sharp part of its beak, is breaking out of its shell. The other eggs begin to hatch, too.

DOWN

A group of newly hatched chicks is called a BROOD.

At first the chicks are wet and sticky. They are very tired. Soon they dry and have fluffy yellow feathers called down. They become stronger. They can see and hear and begin to move about. The chicks make a cheeping sound to let their mother know where they are. The mother hen clucks and drops food in front of them. Chicks can eat the same food as their mothers.

FEATHERS

In a few weeks the chicks are bigger, but their mother still protects them. The chicks have grown feathers. In a few months these young chickens will look like their mother or father. A female chicken will be able to lay her first eggs when she is about 5 months old.

Female chickens less than 6 months old are called pullets. After that they are called hens. Male chickens less than a year old are called cockerels. After that they are called roosters. There are more than ten billion chickens in the world!

GATHERING EGGS ON SMALL FARMS

1. The eggs are gathered by hand twice a day from the hens' nests.

2. The eggs are washed, rinsed, and dried. They are placed in a refrigerator to be kept and used later.

3. Sometimes the owners place the extra eggs into egg cartons to be sold at farm stands.

GATHERING EGGS ON LARGE FARMS

1. The eggs are laid and roll down the sloping floors of the cages.

2. The eggs are washed, rinsed, and dried.

3. Then the eggs are rolled over bright lights. This is called CANDLING. Workers are able to see through the shells to make sure there are no imperfections.

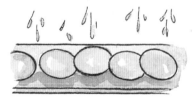

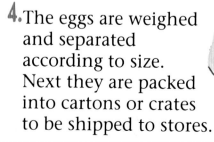

4. The eggs are weighed and separated according to size. Next they are packed into cartons or crates to be shipped to stores.

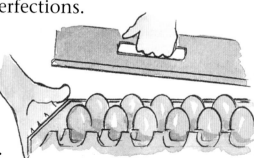

HOW CHICKENS ARE RAISED
ON A LARGE FARM FOR THEIR MEAT

1. Many chickens begin their lives at special farms called chicken hatcheries. These farms often use special machines, called incubators, to keep the eggs warm.

INCUBATOR

2. When the eggs hatch, the chicks are raised in large groups.

3. The chickens live in chicken barns and are fed and given water by machines.

4. At any one time a large commercial farm may have 10,000 to 100,000 chickens.

Mother hens cluck to communicate to their chicks. A deep cluck means "Follow me!" A high-pitched cluck means "Food!" Chicks can recognize their own mother's cluck.

Hens and roosters may live to be about 12 years old.

The heaviest chicken ever weighed, a White Sully, was 22 pounds (9.9 kg).

The shell of an egg is strong. With its pointed end up, it can support up to 9 pounds (4 kg) before breaking.

A miniature chicken of a standard breed is called a bantam.

The most eggs ever laid by a chicken in one year was 371.

The heaviest chicken egg ever weighed was 13 ounces (368.5 g).

The largest chicken egg ever laid was 12 inches (30.4 cm) long.

Each year in the United States about 250 million hens lay about 80 billion eggs.

At Easter some people like dyeing and decorating chicken eggs. There are Easter egg hunts.